Sympathetic Storytelling

How to Connect with Your Audience Through Shared Human Emotions

© Copyright 2017 by Nathan Pengram - All rights reserved.

The transmission, duplication or reproduction of any of the following work including specific information will be considered an illegal act irrespective of if it is done electronically or in print. This extends to creating a secondary or tertiary copy of the work or a recorded copy and is only allowed with an express written consent of the Publisher. All additional right reserved.

The information in the following pages is broadly considered to be a truthful and accurate account of facts and as such any inattention, use or misuse of the information in question by the reader will render any resulting actions solely under their purview. There are no scenarios in which the publisher or the original author of this work can be in any fashion deemed liable for any hardship or damages that may befall them after undertaking information described herein.

Additionally, the information in the following pages is intended only for informational purposes and should thus be thought of as universal. As befitting its nature, it is presented without assurance regarding its prolonged validity or interim quality. Trademarks that are mentioned are done without written consent and can in no way be considered an endorsement from the trademark holder.

The author of this book has taken careful measures to share vital information about the subject. May its readers acquire the right knowledge, wisdom, inspiration, and succeed.

Table of Contents

Introduction 1

Chapter 1: The Basics of Storytelling 3

Chapter 2: Examples and The Methods Behind Them 19

Chapter 3: How to Tell a Story – Your Story 35

Conclusion 59

Introduction

Congratulations on purchasing this book and thank you for doing so.

The following chapters will teach you everything that you need to know about sympathetic storytelling. Whether you want to communicate something more effectively or persuade people to accept your views, learning sympathetic storytelling will allow you to fully harness the power of stories which you can use to your advantage. If you are looking for something that will teach you the ins and outs of storytelling, then this book is for you. Sympathetic storytelling will allow you to connect to your audience through shared human emotions. This is an art that you can apply to your everyday life.

Chapter 1 discusses the basics of storytelling. Before you can start applying your skills as a storyteller, you must first establish a strong foundation and understanding of what sympathetic storytelling is all about.

Chapter 2 gives examples of different stories. Every story is followed by a discussion and analysis for you to understand how sympathetic storytelling is applied, as well as how you can craft a story more effectively.

Chapter 3 lays down the best practices of storytelling. Learn how to tell stories like a master storyteller who can evoke and arouse the emotions of his audience. Turn these practices into a habit, and you will be on your way to becoming a successful storyteller. Including many techniques to improve your storytelling ability and the messages behind the stories themselves.

There are plenty of books on this subject on the market, thanks again for choosing this one! Every effort was made to ensure it is full of as much useful information as possible.

Please enjoy!

Chapter 1
The Basics of Storytelling

Storytelling has long been a part of humanity. But, what is storytelling? Narratives can be found in many different cultures from different parts of the world. Stories have been told through the ages for purposes of education, entertainment, instilling moral values, and for cultural preservation, among others. In a narrow sense, the term *storytelling* may refer to the oral practice of telling stories. These stories may be real or fiction. Of course, storytelling can also be in written form, such as those found in novels and epic poems. It can also take a more visual approach like plays and movies. But, regardless of how it is conveyed, the important thing is that a story is always told, which can be real or imaginary, or even both.

Brief history

It is worth noting that storytelling has long been in existence even before writing was even created. Stories were told by people orally. Storytelling have always been part of religions and rituals. There are also archaeologists who believe that rock art has also been used to tell stories. Archaeologists also discovered paintings on walls which were said to be used by ancient storytellers to help them remember their stories. Drawings on trees, sands, and walls, were also used to tell stories.

When writing was finally developed, stories were converted in written form and were spread throughout various regions of the world. Still, stories that are told orally continued to flourish. Many of these stories have been passed on from generation to generation, and some of them have been transcribed into written form.

There is no record as to the very first story that was told by humanity. After all, stories can be said to be as old as humanity itself, considering that every person always has a story to tell.

Is storytelling important?

Yes, storytelling is important. In fact, it is what preserves the whole human race. As said by a scholar and risk analyst, Nassim Nicholas Taleb, "Ideas come and go, stories stay." Some even say that storytelling is a mark of humanity. After all, everything — from the distant past up to the present moment and the future — is full of stories. Stories are handed down year after year, generation after generation, and always reflect humanity. The stories that you read today are the proof of the many lives that existed before you. The good news is that there is no end to storytelling. It is also not limited to books. Stories are everywhere: on the TV, in the newspapers, magazines, social media channels, lyrics of songs, as a part of a business presentation, and many others. Life is full of stories, and many of them are worth telling and retelling.

What are the applications for storytelling?

Storytelling as an art and a skill can be applied in many ways. As you may already know, storytelling is used to entertain, inform, persuade, instill values, or simply share something with people. Not to mention, there are also those who make a living by telling stories, like novelists and other writers. Stories convey a message to people. If properly told, a story even has the power to change a person, even the world.

Who uses storytelling?

Everybody uses storytelling. If you remember the last time that you spent quality time with your friends, for sure you also exchanged stories with one another. Storytellers are everywhere. They are on TV, websites, magazines, books, and newspapers. Literally, everybody tells a story. Even at an early age, stories are introduced to people. Take, for example, the parents who read fairy tales to their kids in bed. It is also common for business presentations and speeches to have stories in them. Storytelling has a power that is able to relate and connect deeply with another person. But, of course, for this to happen, a person must tell the right story and be able to deliver it effectively.

What is sympathetic storytelling?

Sympathetic storytelling is an effective way to tell a story. It will allow you to connect with another person on a more intimate level. As the term implies, it is a storytelling where feel for and with the audience. Hence, it becomes more intimate and powerful.

You can use sympathetic storytelling to improve your social interaction, conversation, or speech. It will help you express your message clearly and get the message through effectively. Using basic human emotions, the fundamental feelings everyone shares, you can connect with your audience and make them sympathetic, and agree with your view. It is not a quick fix on how to do a cheap trick to manipulate others. It is, in fact, a realization and implementation of your innermost feeling or the feelings and experience of the characters in your stories, as well as finding a common ground with your audience. Amid all the differences, you can capture your audience and make them understand how you or the character in your story feels. It is finding that common past experience the audience can relate to, the same moral ground the audience can stand on. Simply put, it is the kind of storytelling that is powerful, intimate, and effective. It is the way to tell a story that can touch the hearts of the people who listen to it.

Sympathetic storytelling and human emotions

Sympathetic storytelling relates to basic emotions and experiences, such as joy, sadness, fulfillment, duty, morality, gratitude, debt, dignity, making difficult choices, doing the right thing, regret, pain, and overcoming seemingly insurmountable odds to success. By telling a story that connects to a specific emotion, a stronger bond and connection are made with your audience.

Understanding emotion

Did you know that the word "emotion" comes from Latin, which means "to disturb?" If the personality of your characters lies only in the mind or how they think instead of being in their actions and emotions, then it also creates a distance that separates the audience from the story. The thing is that thoughts are not always easy to understand, and even dialogues can sometimes lie.

However, emotions speak a universal language that everybody can understand. It is something that humans know to be real. And, more importantly, emotions do not lie since feelings, even if unreasonable, remain true.

Sympathetic storytelling means so much more than having action pieces and a logical order of events for you to draw logical conclusions. It is true that applying storytelling techniques can make the audience feel more excited about the story. However, they are not enough to hook the audience to your story. If you come to think of it, is it not that the best stories out there are those that have touched you emotionally? This is how powerful emotions are, and it is what creates audience identification.

Even the change that a character goes through is only real and believable only if it affects the character on an emotional level. However, if the character himself does not feel such a strong emotion or does not change even emotionally, then you cannot expect for your story to have a lasting impression on your audience.

Sympathetic storytelling and social interactions

Sympathetic storytelling works well when you are engaged in any social interaction. Whether you are going to deliver a speech in front of a live audience, present a business presentation, or simply when engaged in day-to-day casual conversations, sympathetic storytelling can make all your social interactions more beneficial and interesting.

Stories can have a strong convincing power. Also, some things are better explained by telling a story. For some reason, stories are also easier to remember. It is not uncommon for a good story to remain unforgotten. Of course, stories are one thing, how the stories are told is another. It is important for the elements of a story to have a smooth and perfect flow, and the story has to be delivered in an effective way.

Social interactions present an opportunity to tell a story. You can use a good story to get a message across to another person or a group of people. It is worth noting that sympathetic storytelling is not just any kind of storytelling. As the term implies, you will have to feel for and with your audience. You will use the story and the characters in your story to establish a more intimate connection with your audience.

Elements of a story

Every story has five basic elements:

- characters
- setting
- plot
- conflict
- resolution

These elements give a story a smooth and logical flow, which make it easy for the audience to follow. Let us take a closer look at the elements one by one:

Characters

The characters in a story are the individuals who act in a narrative. It is important that every character is properly introduced so that the audience will be more able to visualize them. This can be done by telling the audience what a character is doing, his or her physical attributes and any personality traits that may be worth telling.

Take note that it is important for every story to have a main character. It is the main character that determines how the plot of the story will be developed and is usually the one who will face any obstacle or problem in the story. So much of your audience's attention will be placed on the main character. In fact, according to a study, the audience usually relate them to the main character in a story. For this reason, you should make your main character interesting enough. Of course, other characters are also important. They can give more details and make developments in the story. Their actions can also have a strong impact on the direction of the story.

The main character refers to the protagonist or the hero in the story. It is worth noting that the protagonist does not always have to be the good guy. He may start as someone with a bad personality but then change into something good. Also, a story can also have more than one main character or protagonists.

A story may or may not have a villain or the enemy of the main character. After all, the challenges in a story can come from various sources, even from the main character himself.

Setting

The setting refers to the place and time where the story takes place. When other people talk about the setting, they sometimes limit it to just the place. This is wrong. Time is also an essential element of any story. For example, New York City today was so much different a century ago. It is a good practice to describe the setting clearly so that the audience can be able to visualize the environment where the actions take place.

Plot

The plot covers the beginning, middle, and end, of the story. Hence, it refers to the story itself, including all the descriptions and suspense, if any. To come up with an interesting story, you need to have an interesting plot.

Conflict

Every story has a conflict. It is also what makes a plot interesting. Conflicts usually come in the form of challenges or obstacles. It can be a conflict between the protagonist (the main character) against other characters. It can also be a conflict between the protagonist against nature, or even against himself. Of course, as you may already know, the most exciting part of a story is called the climax. The climax happens before the resolution.

Resolution

As the name already implies, this refers to the solution the conflict or problem in the story. It is important for the resolution to solve the whole conflict and must be able to fit nicely into the story.

Elements of a plot

The plot is extremely important in every story. It is what dictates the flow of the story, as well as the events that take place therein. There are five elements of a plot:

- beginning
- rising action
- climax
- falling action
- denouement

Take a closer look and understand these elements one by one:

Beginning

The beginning or the exposition of the story is what prepares the interesting events that will happen in the story. This part of the plot is where a storyteller introduces the main characters, the setting of the story, as well as the conflict that the protagonist has to face. This is also the part where you can talk about any back story of a character if any. A good example of an exposition is in the story of "The Adventures of Huckleberry Finn." It is about an adolescent who is not happy with his life as he lives with a widow and does not have a good relationship with his greedy father. The place of the story is in a river town near the Mississippi River. As for the time, the story is set in around 1800s. Indeed, it is a true classic. There is no villain in the story. Instead, the conflict is the protagonist's desire to have an adventure. As part of the exposition to get the story forward, Huck goes on a tumultuous journey on a riverboat.

Rising action

This part of the plot is what leads to the climax (the most exciting part of the story). This is where you build a tension. In "The Maze Runner," the protagonist escapes his old, prison-like experience by entering a maze, as well as to save his friends. It sets the stage for a really intense or exciting event in the story.

Climax

The climax of the story is usually defined as the most exciting part of the story and is also referred to as the turning point of the story. It is usually the most difficult challenge or moment that the protagonist faces. In "The Hunger Games," the climax is when the main characters, Katniss and Peeta, decide not to eat the poisoned berries. They decide to die together instead of killing each other. It is the turning point and most interesting moment of a story.

Falling action

The falling action takes place after the climax. It is the consequence of the actions of the protagonist during the climax, whether good or bad. This usually sets the stage for the resolution or ending of the story. In "How to Kill a Mockingbird," the falling action is when Bob (antagonist) attacks two of the protagonists, Scout and Jem — the children are then saved by the town recluse by killing Ewell. If you know the story, then it is not hard to realize that this is just a mere consequence of what happens in the climax of the same story. Simply put, the falling action answers the "what happens now?" right after the climax, which then leads to the resolution or final chapter.

Resolution

This is the ending of the story. Here, the conflicts have all been resolved, and everything has been answered — except in case of a sequel where there will be a room for more plot developments. It is worth noting that not all stories have a good and happy ending. Some stories have a sad ending. In fact, there are also stories that do not actually have a clear ending but leaves to the audience to decide what happens in the end. This is often referred to as an open ending. Simply put, this part of the resolution is the ending of a story.

Audience empathy

Sympathetic storytelling also follows all the elements of a story and a plot. However, it also exercises what is called as audience empathy. What is audience empathy? It is the ability to understand and have compassion for the state of mind of your audience, as well as how they feel about your story. This makes you aware and have more control of their emotional state.

Why is it important to connect with your audience's emotion? According to research, most people respond in accordance with how they feel — their emotion. They only use logic or reasons to justify their actions, but emotion remains to be the leading and moving element of everything in a story. It is also by tapping your audience's emotional state that you can make them respond in your favor. It is also by understanding how your audience feels that you can use the most effective and appropriate story to tell.

This applies even in business. Remember Procter and Gamble's campaign called, "Thank you, Mom." It was a big hit. The reason is that the campaign made its way into the hearts of many mothers in the world by acknowledging the jobs that mothers do every day. There is appreciation for their hard work, which oftentimes is taken for granted or not completely appreciated.

What do you want your audience to feel?

When it comes to sympathetic storytelling, you should ask yourself this question: What do I want my audience to feel? Whatever emotion it is, you will then use that emotion to be the central force of your story. For example, if it is love, then you will come up with a central force that is on the theme of love or evokes the energy of love. If the emotion or idea that you want to feed to your audience is about pursuing one's dream, then let your story revolve around such theme.

Okay, by now you should have an emotion that you want your audience to feel. However, the question remains: How do you effectively communicate this emotion to your audience? There are many ways to do this when you do storytelling. However, if you find it hard to express a particular emotion effectively, a good tip is to focus on your protagonist. People usually identify themselves with the protagonist to the point that they get to feel what the protagonist feels in the story. Or, more specifically, they feel for the protagonist — they empathize with him. Hence, by using your protagonist, you can more easily communicate a feeling or emotion to your audience. Another helpful tip is to simply communicate an emotion that your audience already has. For example, if the friend with whom you are talking to is in love, then you can tell him about a good love story that will further inspire the emotion that he is already feeling.

Shared human emotion

Sympathetic storytelling takes advantage of shared human emotion to increase the power and effectiveness of a story. What is this "shared human emotion"? Simply put, it refers to any emotion that is shared or experienced by the storyteller and the audience. It is this commonality that creates a better and more intimate bond through the story. Take note, however, that as a storyteller, you do not always need to have a first-hand experience of the emotion. Therefore, even if you have not personally experienced a particular emotion, does not mean that you cannot tell a good story about it. In such cases, sympathetic storytellers learn to adapt the emotion for the sake of telling a good story sympathetically.

So, how does this work? For example, if you are going to tell a story about love but you have not fallen in love before, a sympathetic storyteller may fill his mind with stories of love. Hence, he may read and watch love stories, even analyze some love poems, and others. In other words, he can fill his consciousness with things that talk about love. Once he feels this love, he can then express this love and connect with people who may share the same emotion. Of course, as a storyteller, you should not allow yourself to be limited by your environment or your personal experiences. Your imagination remains the most powerful tool that you can use to craft a story. In fact, just by exercising your imagination and exploring the inner realms inside your mind, there is no emotion that will be a stranger to you. This is one of the best things about sympathetic storytelling. You do not just tell a story. Rather, you also feel the story, which can even create positive changes in you.

Why Storytelling works

Storytelling works. Whether you want to use it to give new information, persuade an audience, entertainment, to teach something, or even if you simply want to share something — storytelling can make you communicate it more effectively. Humans have been telling stories since the dawn of time. Unlike watching a movie, stories make use of the imagination. And, as you may already know, once you get deep into a person's imagination, you get into his mind. Once you are in a person's mind, you can make him see and experience remarkable things.

Various studies and experiments have also been conducted as to how effective storytelling can be. It was found that a different area of the brain that relates to empathy and feeling when one listens to a good story than merely listening or reading facts. It can be said that storytelling or listening to stories is more human in the sense that it involves the emotions and allows a man to "feel."

Chapter 2
Examples and The Methods Behind Them

Using sympathetic storytelling is an effective way to communicate something to your audience. Let us look at some samples and applications of sympathetic storytelling:

"*I heard a nice little story the other day,*" *Morrie says. He closes his eyes for a moment and I wait.*

"*Okay. The story is about a little wave, bobbing along in the ocean, having a grand old time. He's enjoying the wind and the fresh air-- until he notices the other waves in front of him, crashing against the shore.*"

"*'My God, this is terrible,' the wave says 'Look what's going to happen to me!'*"

"*Then along comes another wave. It sees the first wave looking grim, and it says to him, 'Why do you look so sad?'*"

"*The first wave says, 'You don't understand! We're all going to crash! All of us waves are going to be nothing! Isn't it terrible?'*"

"*The second wave says, 'No, you don't understand. You're not a wave, you're part of the ocean.'*" —*Tuesdays with Morrie by Mitch Albom*

This is a story about death and spirituality. Of course, you can tell this story if it is relevant to the mood or topic of a situation. As you can see, when you use stories, you do not always have to use real people. You are free to illustrate your point using other things, in this case, two waves and an ocean. You can also notice the plot here clearly. Although it is a very short story, it satisfies all the elements of a story. The setting is in the ocean. The characters are the two waves in the ocean. The conflict is that they are surely both going to crash against the shore and "die." Of course, the line that marks the point or lesson of the story is found in the last line where the second wave says, "No, you don't understand. You're not a wave, you're part of the ocean." There seems to be no better way to illustrate what Morrie was trying to say except with the use of a story — this story. The more that this appeals to the emotion considering that Morrie was already dying when he told this story. It is no secret that the topic of death or dying is of common interest to everyone since everyone is headed towards the same direction. The key to sympathetic story telling is to identify a specific topic or emotion and come up with a story that connects to it. The audience will be able to connect to it on their own without you having to explain every point or symbolism in the story. The reason is because they feel it with you. But, of course, before you can come up with such story, you need to feel it first and then share that emotion that the audience also feels. You summon and strengthen that emotion with your story.

Take a look at another story, or rather, a speech. Pay attention to how the speech tells a story by recounting the past and giving hope to the present:

"Four score and seven years ago our fathers brought forth on this continent, a new nation, conceived in Liberty, and dedicated to the proposition that all men are created equal.

Now we are engaged in a great civil war, testing whether that nation, or any nation so conceived and so dedicated, can long endure. We are met on a great battle-field of that war. We have come to dedicate a portion of that field, as a final resting place for those who here gave their lives that that nation might live. It is altogether fitting and proper that we should do this.

But, in a larger sense, we cannot dedicate -- we cannot consecrate -- we cannot hallow -- this ground. The brave men, living and dead, who struggled here, have consecrated it, far above our poor power to add or detract. The world will little note, nor long remember what we say here, but it can never forget what they did here. It is for us the living, rather, to be dedicated here to the unfinished work which they who fought here have thus far so nobly advanced. It is rather for us to be here dedicated to the great task remaining before us -- that from these honored dead we take increased devotion to that cause for which they gave the last full measure of devotion -- that we here highly resolve that these dead shall not have died in vain -- that this nation, under God, shall have a new birth of freedom -- and that government of the people, by the people, for the people, shall not perish from the earth." —Abraham Lincoln, November 19, 1863

Known as the Gettysburg Address, this speech changed a whole nation. There are strong sympathy and appeal to the emotion. The speech reminds the audience of immeasurable sacrifices and meaning. The words and the flow of the lines are also well made. And, since this speech was first recited by the American President, Abraham Lincoln, you can be rest assured that it was properly addressed and delivered. The beginning of the line mentions a setting in terms of date. Take note that a score is equivalent to 20 years. Hence, if you do the computation, he was, in fact, recalling the time of Declaration of Independence. He then went on to recall the sacrifices that were made to achieve independence. Of course, he relayed this message to the right people: the people of America. The speech then ends with a call to action, "These dead shall not have died in vain -- that this nation, under God, shall have a new birth of freedom -- and that government of the people, by the people, for the people, shall not perish from the earth."

Here is another interesting story. Many motivational speakers use this as an introduction to their actual speech:

A famous speaker started his seminar by showing a $100 bill in a room of 100 people, and asked, "Who would like this $100 bill?"

Hands started going up.

He said, "I am going to give this $100 bill to one of you, but first let me do this...."

He started to crumple the $100 bill.

He then asked, "Who still wants it?"

Still, the hands were up in the air.

"Well".... he replied,

"What if I do this?".... and he dropped the bill on the ground and started to grind it into the floor with his shoe.

He picked it up, now crumpled and dirty. "Now who still wants it?" he asked. And hands were still in the air.

"My friends, you have all learned a very valuable lesson. No matter what I did to the money, you still wanted it...because it did not decrease in value. It was still worth $100."

In life, sometimes we suddenly get dropped and crumpled like dirt because of the decisions that we make, as well as the circumstances that come our way.

During such times, we cannot help but feel worthless. But, always keep in mind that no matter what happens, you will always be valuable.

The people who truly care about you will always love you even when you see yourself as clean, dirty, or crumpled. You will always be priceless.

The worth of our lives comes not in what we do or who we know, but by WHO WE ARE.

You are, and will always be, special. No matter what people tell you. Never forget about it.

The following story is an excellent example of sympathetic storytelling. It is a good story to use when you want to talk about kindness or being kind despite being treated unjustly:

One day, there was a Hindu who saw a scorpion floundering around a water. He wanted to save it by stretching out his finger, but the scorpion stung him. Again, he extended his finger to save the scorpion, but it stung him for the second time. A man who was nearby saw what he was doing and asked him why he kept saving the scorpion that kept on stinging him. To this, the Hindu replied, "It is in the nature of the scorpion to sting. It is my nature to love. Why would I give up my nature to love just because it is the nature of the scorpion to sting?" The lesson of the story: Do not give up kindness. Do not give up your goodness, even when people around you sting.

As you can see in the story, the storyteller uses the character of a scorpion to symbolize a bad person or bad people. It is common knowledge that scorpions sting. In the story, it is the act of stinging that is used to signify a person who does bad things, which also "sting." The Hindu represents a good person. The story captures the attention easily because it uses something that seems absurd whereby the Hindu keeps saving a scorpion that keeps hurting him. In other words, a person who continuously loves someone who keeps hurting him. This is a very curious thing, even when you think about it right now. Of course, this is not just about capturing attention. Creativity must also coincide with logic. Hence, a reason is given to defend the "absurd" act of saving the scorpion. The story also ends beautifully by giving a short yet clear explanation: *"The lesson of the story: Do not give up kindness. Do not give up your goodness, even when people around you sting."*

Take a look at another story that is usually shared by motivational speakers:

As a man was passing by, he saw some elephants, and stopped, confused by the fact that these huge animals were being held by only a small rope tied to their front leg. No chains, no cages. It was obvious that the elephants could, at any time, break away from their bonds but for some reason, they did not.

He saw a trainer nearby and asked why these animals just stood there and made no attempt to get away. "Well," trainer said, "when they are very young and much smaller we use the same size rope to tie them and, at that age, it's enough to hold them. As they grow up, they are conditioned to believe they cannot break away. They believe the rope can still hold them, so they never try to break free."

The man was amazed. The animals could actually break free from their bonds. However, because they believed they couldn't, they were stuck right where they were.

Just like these elephants, there are many people who continue to hold on to a belief that they cannot do something just because they failed at it before. Keep in mind that failing is a normal part of the learning process. Therefore, you should not give up no matter what struggle you may face in life.

Take note that this story is just a short one, which can be said in a few minutes. Many speakers use it in the beginning of a speech or even in the middle of a speech. Since it is only a short story, the details must be expressed concisely using as few words as possible.

The first line makes a quick introduction. The first paragraph also compels the audience to wonder: *"It was obvious that the elephants could, at any time, break away from their bonds but for some reason, they did not."* It is followed by another paragraph where another character is presented in order to explain the seeming mystery with the elephants. It is a natural and important transition to get the story forward. It is followed by another paragraph, which is the falling action.

The story then transitions to a more practical and clearer meaning: *"Like the elephants, how many of us go through life hanging onto a belief that we cannot do something, simply because we failed at it once before?"* This part is also more directed to the audience. Last but not least, it concludes with a life's lesson that anyone can surely relate to: *"Failure is part of learning; we should never give up the struggle in life."*

Not all stories that you tell should be fiction. As they say, real life can sometimes be stranger than fiction. Therefore, it is also good to tell about real-life stories from time to time. If you have a friend who is facing problems or rejections, then the following story may help lift his courage and make him more inspired. It is another story that is used by storytellers. Although its original author remains unknown, it is widely circulated online. And, of course, it is a true story:

"Once, there was an older man, who was broke, living in a tiny house and owned a beat-up car. He was living off of $99 social security checks. At 65 years of age, he decided things had to change. So, he thought about what he had to offer. His friends raved about his chicken recipe. He decided that this was his best shot at making a change.

He left Kentucky and traveled to different states to try to sell his recipe. He told restaurant owners that he had a mouthwatering chicken recipe. He offered the recipe to them for free, just asking for a small percentage of the items sold. Sounds like a good deal, right?

Unfortunately, not to most of the restaurants. He heard NO over 1000 times. Even after all of those rejections, he didn't give up. He believed his chicken recipe was something special. He got rejected 1009 times before he heard his first yes.

With that one success, Colonel Harland Sanders changed the way Americans eat chicken. Kentucky Fried Chicken, popularly known as KFC, was born.

Remember, never give up and always believe in yourself in spite of rejection."

The story begins with a humble introduction of the protagonist. The first paragraph also emphasizes the challenges faced by the main character. But, it also reveals a solution or simply an action that he can take. It is followed by another paragraph which seems to only show that the character in the story has decided to pursue the action. However, if you look closely, it also mentions for the first time the word "Kentucky," which is a foreshadowing of the identity of the protagonist, as will be completely revealed in the last paragraph of the story.

The story continues to show that challenges and rejection do not seem to stop. This part of the story actually encourages the audience to listen more and find out what will happen in the story. After all, the protagonist seems to be being defeated over and over again. A good twist has to happen. It then uses a paragraph that not only highlights the success of the protagonist but also gives a surprising revelation as to who the character is in real life: "With that one success Colonel Harland Sanders changed the way Americans eat chicken. Kentucky Fried Chicken, popularly known as KFC, was born."

Although the story talks about the life of a real person, the lesson in the story can be understood and even felt by other people, which gives it a fine conclusion: "Remember, never give up and always believe in yourself in spite of rejection."

Here is another fine story that you can share with anyone who might be having problems or facing difficulties in life. It is about being creative and thinking "outside of the box" to solve a problem:

"Years ago, in a humble Italian town, there was a small business owner who owed a large sum of money to a loan-shark. The loan-shark was an old and unattractive guy who happened to fancy the daughter of the business owner.

To wipe out the debt, he offered a deal to the businessman. However, there was a catch: That the debt will only be removed if he marries the businessman's daughter. Needless to say, the catch was looked at with disgust.

The loan-shark said that a white and black pebble will be placed in a bag. The daughter would then have to reach into the bag and pick out a pebble. If she picked the black stone, then the debt will be removed, but she will have to marry him, the loan-shark. However, if she picked the white stone, then the debt would also be wiped out, but this time, the daughter would not have to marry the loan-shark.

Standing on a pebble-strewn path in the businessman's garden, the loan-shark bent over and picked up two pebbles. While he was picking them up, the daughter noticed that he had picked up two black pebbles and placed them both into the bag. He then asked the daughter to reach into the bag and pick one.

The daughter naturally had three choices as to what she could have done:

1. *Refuse to pick a pebble from the bag.*
2. *Take both pebbles out of the bag and expose the loan-shark for cheating.*

3. *Pick a pebble from the bag fully well knowing it was black and sacrifice herself for her father's freedom.*

She drew out a pebble from the bag, and before looking at it 'accidentally' dropped it into the midst of the other pebbles. She said to the loan-shark; "Oh, How clumsy of me. Never mind, if you look into the bag for the one that is left, you will be able to tell which pebble I picked.

The pebble left in the bag is obviously black, and seeing as the loan-shark didn't want to be exposed, he had to play along as if the pebble the daughter dropped was white, and clear her father's debt."

This story is really good. It does not just sympathize with the emotion of an audience but also leads their thoughts. A problem is presented. The story also mentions the possible and logical solutions to the problem. It would appear for a moment that there is no way to win against the loan-shark in the story. This is a perfect example of using a story to connect with a real-life situation that your audience can relate to. Do you remember the times when you faced obstacles that you thought you could not overcome or problems that could not be resolved? The story will definitely remind you of such situation and offers a solution. It does not necessarily offer the solution to your problem per se, but it can give you hope and inspiration that you can definitely understand.

This is one of the secrets of sympathetic storytelling. It does not talk about a certain topic directly but uses examples that are related to real-life experiences. And, if the audience has experienced a similar situation in life or at least the emotion that the said situation evokes, then they will surely be able to sympathize with the story.

Let us examine another story entitled, "Harry Potter." Harry is a young wizard who is a student in a school of wizardry, Hogwarts. His parents were killed by a powerful and dark wizard named, Voldemort. It is a story that is beyond the ordinary world where there are monsters, magic spells, and potions. Still, people are able to deeply connect to it and sympathize with the characters.

Let us take a closer look at the protagonist, Harry, and find out why the audience is drawn to his character, as well as to the story itself.

Background

Harry Potter has a different background from an average Joe. He is young with magical powers. His parents were killed when he was still a baby. He lived with his close relatives who did not treat him nicely. It was in Hogwarts where he found his real home.

Ability

Harry Potter is a wizard, so he has many magical abilities. He can also talk to snakes. Although not considered a magical ability, Harry is known for being a very kind and truthful person.

Social

The life of Harry Potter is not just about magic. It is also about friendship. He has two close friends: Hermione Granger and Ron

Weasley. He is also kind and nice to everyone. Friendship is also the central theme of the movie.

How are they connected?

You might be wondering: Where is the connection between Harry Potter and the audience? Take note that Harry goes through different emotions in the story. For example, he has strong desires to see and talk with his parents. Also, the value of friendship is one of the main highlights of the story. In the story, Harry always does his best to help his friends. People are able to understand and sympathize with these emotions; therefore, even though Harry Potter's background may not be the same as everyone else, the emotions evoked in the story allow the character to connect with the viewer or reader on a more intimate level — so much so that they get to like the protagonist to the point that they want him to succeed.

Let us take a look at another story: *Fifty Shades of Grey*. This erotic and romance story gained worldwide popularity. It is a story of a literature student Anastasia Steele who goes to interview a prominent business magnate, Christian Grey, a beautiful, brilliant, and intimidating man. The unworldly, innocent Ana is startled to realize she wants this man and, despite his enigmatic reserve, finds she is desperate to get close to him. Unable to resist Ana's quiet beauty, wit, and independent spirit, Grey admits he wants her, too—but on his own terms. They end up having a sexual affair. They fall in love with each other as she discovers his "dark" side.

Let us look at the character of Anastasia Steele:

Background

Anastasia Steele is a literature student. Unlike Christian Grey, she has no sexual experience — a virgin. She is also not wealthy. She is presented as an ordinary girl who is into literature, which means that she has a heart. And, when it comes to sexual matters, she is completely innocent, while Christian Grey is someone who is very much experienced in sex and has strong sexual urges.

Financial standing

Anastasia Steele is not a rich person. She is presented as a typical woman, while Christian Grey is a rich and prominent businessman. Being an ordinary woman, many will be able to easily relate to the character of Anastasia.

Ability

The story does not show that Anastasia possesses any notable or unusual ability. However, she is the only one who makes Christian Grey fall in love.

So, how does the story draw the attention and interest of its readers/viewers? Again, it is the emotion. Therefore, even if you do not have the same background as Anastasia Steele, you will be able to easily connect and sympathize with her, much more if you have a similar background. As for the men, they can always relate themselves to Christian Grey in the story. And, since sex is a primary theme of the story, every human being is able to relate to it. Also, in the story, Christian Grey is presented as someone who is rich and strong. He also uses women to satisfy his sexual urges.

But then he falls in love with Anastasia. The story deals with romance and lust, which are both interesting topics for many people. When Anastasia decides to sign the contract, and have a sexual affair with Mr. Grey, it speaks directly to those women who surrender themselves to their partners.

The story also plays with a woman's fantasy in the person of Christian Grey. He is rich, decent, smart, and handsome. He is the perfect partner for a woman. However, he has a serious flaw that Anastasia has to accept. The viewers, especially the women, are easily able to sympathize with this because they have also experienced accepting the imperfections and flaws of their partner in real life.

Notes

Study these stories carefully. Pay attention to how the events transition from one another, the flow of the story, as well as how the emotions of the characters are able to connect with the audience. As you can see, sympathetic storytelling is not a new concept. People have been telling such stories for ages. However, what makes sympathetic storytelling different lies in your ability to discern what story to tell, when to tell the story, and how to deliver it effectively. To do this, you need to empathize with your audience and use characters in the story that the audience can sympathize with. This way, a strong and intimate connection can be made between you, the story, and your audience.

Chapter 3
How to Tell a Story – Your Story

The important thing about sympathetic storytelling is that you tell a story. But, it cannot just be any kind of story. It must be something that can connect with your audience on a more personal level. But, how do you tell such kind of a good story? Indeed, anyone can tell a story at any moment like, for example, the story about your first day in the school or at work. However, being a sympathetic storyteller means so much more than telling a story. There are two things to take note of, the particular story that you will tell, as well as how you will deliver or tell the story. To be an effective storyteller, you need to learn the best practices of sympathetic storytellers, so that you will be able to communicate your message clearly to your audience.

Show; don't tell

This is a common advice given to would-be storytellers. Use words that will show what happens in the story instead of telling everything. Trust your audience or readers' imagination. Instead of saying that Sandra is very sad, you can say that Sandra's eyes are swollen with tears. Showing instead of telling makes the story and the words more interesting to your audience.

Take note that an important part of storytelling is to get into the mind, or more specifically, the imagination of your audience. Hence, you must be able to control and project certain images to their mind. The problem with simply telling what is happening in the story (instead of showing) is that it does not engage the imagination effectively. Therefore, make it a habit to show by using appropriate descriptions and trust that your audience will get your message. Of course, be sure that you also make the image clear; otherwise, your audience may not be able to get the right idea that you are trying to communicate.

Although this is a sound advice, it is worth noting that this does not apply all the time. There are times when you simply must tell something in order to get a message across quickly. This is true, especially if you only have a limited time to deliver a speech, or if you are just having a casual talk on the elevator. Also, some parts of a story, although important to be mentioned, may not be as interesting. Therefore, you need to be able to communicate these parts without spending too much time with them.

Tell the right story to the right audience

Every story revolves around a specific theme or topic. It is important that you tell a story to the right people — the ones who would relate and empathize with it. For example, you do not tell a love story to someone who is not interested in the idea of love. Rather, what you can do is to use a love story to communicate an idea that the person can empathize with.

As you can see in the previous chapter, the stories deal with a particular point or lesson. It is important that you use the stories on the right occasions. They are not stories that you can tell at any given moment. They have to fit into the situation. For sympathetic storytelling to be successful, a strong connection has to be made.

For this to be possible, the audience has to be able to connect with your story. Hence, they should be interested in your story. For this to happen, your story has to be able to connect to a human emotion that your audience can relate to.

The good news is that there are many raw human emotions that all people can understand and feel. This gives you much flexibility with the story that you can share with an audience. However, it is an advantage if you share something that your audience is already interested in. By doing so, your audience will be able to sympathize with the characters in your story more easily, because he is already connected to the topic of your story in the first place. This will make storytelling much easier.

Proper length

The length of a story also varies depending on the occasion. There are stories that can be shared in less than a minute, while there are also stories that take hours to finish.

The length of the story depends on how much time you have to tell a story. For example, if you are going to deliver a speech in front of an audience, you can use sympathetic storytelling as an introduction or to illustrate an idea. Sometimes things are best understood through stories. It is also a good practice to be concise or to deliver a message or describe something using as little words as possible. This can get you more time to tell your story.

Right characters

The characters in your story, especially the protagonist, should be likable. This means that the audience should like the protagonist in a way that they would want him to succeed. Accordingly, the villain in the story, if any, should project the opposite emotion. Having the right characters is also important because they are the ones who move the storyline. The characters are the actors that make something happen. As a storyteller, you should also have a good understanding of every character and do not make them take unusual actions that are not in line with their personality. Your characters should be believable.

Giving a personality or characterization also gives your audience something to expect. For example, if you characterize the protagonist as a poor man, then the audience will not expect him to be able to buy luxurious items or cars.

Take note that a story may be composed of different characters. Every character should help develop the story. In fact, other storytellers' advice that if a certain character does not in any way develop the story or adds any value to its quality, then it would be better to just remove the said character from the story completely. Therefore, be careful with the characters that you place in your story. Do not forget that even a single character can have a strong impact on the direction of the story.

Compelling plot

The plot of the story should be compelling enough to draw the interest of the audience. The beginning of the story should be catchy enough that people would want to know what will happen in the story. Of course, a good plot means so much more than having an interesting beginning. Every part of the plot must work together to drive the story forward.

But, how do you come up with an interesting plot? A good way, to begin with, is to have an outline where you give a certain complication followed by the way to resolve it in the story. Simply put, your character in the story must want something; however, there must be something that prevents him from having it — the conflict. The question here is: How can the character overcome the obstacle and obtain what he wants? There are other storytellers who do not like to make an outline of a plot because they think that making an outline will only impose a limitation on their creativity. This is not true. An outline assures that your story will stay within the topic and not go far off and be confusing. Do not worry; you do not have to stick to your plot outline completely. Instead, you can use it as a guide to "plot" the whole story.

Once you have a plot outline, it is time to add the characters to bring the plot alive. Take note that the characters are the driving force of a story. It is what they say or do that develops a story. The more colorful your characters are, the more they can capture the attention of the audience. Feel free to exercise your creativity but do not lose focus on the direction of the story. Also, keep in mind that every part of the story matters. Make sure that every scene helps to develop the story.

You would not want to disappoint your audience by giving them a flat and boring ending. Since they have followed your story from the beginning, it is time to give them a satisfying resolution of the story and make all their efforts to listen much worth it. It is time to tie up all the loose ends and be sure to give them a powerful resolution that they will love. Nothing is more disappointing than following a story only to end up with a bad and unsatisfying ending. Many storytellers pay so much attention to building the climax and focus less on what happens after it. Do not be like them. Instead, make sure that the falling action remains as interesting as when you are building a climax. Of course, all these lead to the resolution. Make sure to give your story a beautiful ending that your audience will not forget.

It is also worth noting that the resolution of a story should not take too long right after the climax. Hence, wrap up the story as quickly and neatly as possible. Do not attempt to drag the story longer. Also, remember that how you end of the story should leave a lasting impression on the mind of your audience. Go back and take a look at the example stories in the previous chapter. Do you notice something with how every story ends? Every good story ends with a natural stop and almost always leaves a good and lasting impression.

Another note on how to create a good plot is not to rely on nature or other uncontrollable things to be the one to solve the conflict. The solution to the problem should always come from the character in the story. Of course, some external forces can help, but the main driving force to solve the conflict should always come from the character or protagonist in the story. After all, the audience will not be drawn towards the protagonist if the protagonist himself is not the one who solves the problem in the story.

Last but not least, remember that coming up with a good plot is not always easy. You may have to run a series of trial and error just to find one that would suit your taste and one that your audience will relate to and like. Also, do not think that a good plot has to be complicated. In fact, many wonderful stories have a simple plot. Just trust your imagination and your creativity, and you will soon be able to create a nice plot for a story.

Interesting dialogues

Storytelling is not just about telling a story. Another thing that matters is how you tell the story. Dialogues move a narrative. How the characters talk also show their personality. Hence, you should be careful with your choice of words. Since every character in a story has a different personality, they should not talk in the same way. For example, you should be able to tell that the story uses a demon and a priest through their dialogues and choice of words.

Conflict

The conflict or problem in a story should be something that your audience can relate to. After all, your aim is to use sympathetic storytelling; therefore, it is important that the conflict that you present in your story should be something that your audience will find relevant — something that they can easily relate to. It is worth noting that sympathetic storytelling works even for day-to-day conversations. It is not uncommon for people to talk about problems. If you know good stories or make up your own that can help offer a solution to a problem, then you can use those stories to help someone or better illustrate your idea.

When you do sympathetic storytelling, you should use a conflict that your audience will be able to relate to. You can then charge it with an emotion that your audience will also feel when faced with such conflict.

Foreshadowing

Foreshadowing may not always work in every situation, but it is one of the skills of a good storyteller. It is a literary device in which you give a hint to the audience on what will happen in the story. What makes it tricky is that the audience usually overlooks the hint thinking that it has no significance — until it finally takes place, which can be a big surprise or amazement for the audience.

Take note that foreshadowing is not that simple to do. It takes skill and practice to master the art of foreshadowing. This technique is usually placed in the beginning of a story or even somewhere in the middle while the audience is more focused on something else. A simple example of foreshadowing would be opening a drawing and seeing a magnifying glass beside a gun. This may foreshadow danger. Great storytellers have also used foreshadowing. In fact, even in the story of Romeo and Juliet, as written by William Shakespeare, there is also foreshadowing. If you remember the balcony scene where Juliet fears for Romeo that he might get caught and killed by her kinsmen, there is a line there in a dialogue that says, "My life was better ended by their hate than death prorogued, wanting of thy love." And, as you may already know their story, they soon committed suicide because their families could not accept their love for each other.

If you know Charles Dickens' story entitled *Great Expectation*, then you probably know the foreshadowing there which uses the weather to foreshadow the changes that will happen in the life of Pip:

"Stormy and wet, stormy and wet; and mud, mud, mud, deep in all the streets. Day after day, a vast heavy veil had been driving over London from the East, and it drove still as if in the East there were an Eternity of cloud and wind. So furious had been the gusts, that high buildings in town had had the lead stripped off their roofs; and in the country, trees had been torn up, and sails of windmills carried away; and gloomy accounts had come in from the coast, of shipwreck and death. Violent blasts of rain had accompanied these rages of wind, and the day just closed as I sat down to read had been the worst of all."

Interesting beginning

The beginning, including the opening lines, of your story should be compelling enough for the audience to show interest. Keep in mind that once the audience lost interest in your story, it would be almost impossible to get their interest back. The reason is that even if they suddenly give the story another chance and take notice of it for the second time, it would already be too late for them to follow and understand the whole story. By that time, they will most likely miss out some nice scenes and happenings in your story.

So, how do you start a story in a way that it will capture the interest and attention of your audience? The key is to use the sympathetic approach. Identify a human emotion that your audience will take interest and inject that energy into the story. Another way is to make the audience wonder and use an absurd beginning, such as in the story of *The Towers of Trebizond*. Said story uses an absurd beginning, which is an effective way to make the audience wonder: *"Take my camel, dear,' said my Aunt Dot, as she climbed down from this animal on her return from High Mass."* It can also take a sarcastic approach like in the story written by Jane Austen entitled, *Pride and Prejudice*: *"It is a truth universally acknowledged, that a single man in possession of a good fortune, must be in want of a wife."* Another effective way to begin a story, especially when engaged in a social interaction is by asking a question that the audience will show interest in answering. For example: Do you know what is the meaning of life according to the Shamans? If the audience or the person you are talking to shows interest, then you can follow up the question with your story.

Know what you want to communicate

Before you tell a story or before you even come up with any story, you need to have a clear objective of what you want to communicate with your audience. What human emotion is your story going to connect with and what do you want your audience to feel and learn from the story? You cannot just tell any story that you know. Make sure that what you want to communicate will be interesting to your audience.

Add a personal touch

Although stories can be based on your real life, or they may even be completely taken from your real-life experiences, it is also common to tell stories that are completely fiction in nature. In such case, it is also good to add a personal touch to it by adding something about your life. This will not only make your story more interesting, but it can also make the story more understandable to your audience. A good way to do this is to share something, which may be fictional, and then follow it up with your own real-life experience that is connected to the story. Do not forget to show how the fiction story applies in real-life by using yourself as an example.

Another way to add a personal touch is to change the name or names of the characters in the story and use the names of the people in the audience. Since you are using their names, they would be more interested in finding out what will happen to the characters. Just be careful when you do this. Be sure not to insult or embarrass anyone.

Effective delivery

This is an important part of storytelling. As a sympathetic storyteller, you need to deliver the story in the most effective way. But, what is effective delivery? How can you be sure that the audience is able to connect with your story and vice versa?

There are certain points that you need to consider:

- Have the right story to tell
- Smooth delivery
- Sympathize

No matter how interesting and emphatic your story may be, you cannot expect it to lead to a positive outcome if it is a story that does not relate well to the present situation. For example, you do not tell a romantic story if the focus of the conversation is on running a business. Instead, you need to use a story that is responsive to the situation. Take note that the right story is not necessarily the story that you want to tell. To be more effective, you need to take a shift of perspective and see things from your audience's view. If you were the audience, what story would you like to hear? You need to sympathize with your audience. Telling a story is an act of giving. And, just like giving anything in life, you need to know what it is that you should give. It is something that the audience needs. Hence, focus on your audience. The right story is what your audience needs to hear.

Next, you need to deliver your story smoothly. This also means that you should be able to tell the story clearly. Avoid being like those people who are so disorganized in their thoughts that they fail to tell the story in proper sequence. Do not also be like those who try to remember the story only when they need it already. When it comes to effective storytelling, practice is important. Practice telling your stories until you are able to tell them comfortably and smoothly. Also use good rhythm in telling a story. Rhythm is important. If you only use a steady and unchanging tone, you can expect for your audience to soon get bored and even sleepy. To avoid this from happening, as well as to make the story more interesting, you should adopt a good rhythm. Take note that a good rhythm does not follow a steady flow. Hence, the tone of your voice should change in accordance with the happenings in the story. Learn when to use a low voice and a loud voice. A good way to test your rhythm is to record yourself as you tell the story. You then listen to the recording and see if your rhythm is good enough.

Of course, you need to sympathize with your audience. This is something that you should learn to do the whole time. It is important that you feel for and with your audience. This will give you a better understanding of what they need, which will lead to identifying the right story to tell them. You should also sympathize while you tell the story. This is to increase the interaction rate. Have you noticed those master storytellers who are able to interact with their audience and make them react in the way that he wants them to respond? The reason why they are able to do this is because they are able to sympathize with the people. By sympathizing with your audience, you will be more able to understand them. Once you have a better understanding of your audience, you will then be able to know the best story to tell them, as well as the best approach to tell the story. This is another reason why it is good to have more than one story for a particular human emotion.

Sometimes the kind of story that the audience wants to hear may vary. It is not uncommon for a group to prefer one story over another even though both stories talk about the same subject. Yet you may also find an audience that would prefer the other story, which the other group did not prefer. To know which of the two stories you should tell, you need to empathize with your audience to know which one they would like better.

This sympathy should also extend to the character in the story. You should make the audience see and feel the human emotion involved in the story. A good way to do this is by having the main character in the story be faced with something that the audience is facing or feeling. Do not forget that the audience usually relate themselves to the main character of a story. Therefore, if you are able to present a protagonist that is facing something that is currently being faced by your audience (or anyone who may be listening to you), then they will automatically be able to sympathize with your protagonist. And, what is more, they will be very much interested in your story.

Smooth flow

The parts and events of the story must transition smoothly. This is to avoid confusing your audience. It is also important that the sequence of the event in the story follows a smooth and logical flow.

It is not just the story, but also how you tell the story that should be made in a smooth manner. Also, to ensure the continuous flow of the story, you need to continuously keep your audience interested in what you are saying. You can do this by using grabbing words or details from time to time, such that your audience will wonder as to what will happen next in the story.

Connect with your audience

Sympathetic storytelling is not just about exercising sympathy with your audience through your story, but it is building a strong and intimate connection with them. Hence, as much as possible, try to connect with your audience.

Find out how your audience feel or what could be on their mind. By paying attention to your audience, you will be more able to know how to react appropriately. If engaged in a social interaction, pay attention to their words and gestures. The important thing here is to know the kind of thoughts that are in their mind, as well as to know how they feel. Once you have such information and understanding, then you will know the best story to tell, as well as how you can tell it in the most effective manner.

You should work on intensifying this connection during the speech. You should spellbind them with your interesting plot and deliver the story effectively. When you sympathize with your audience, you can understand how they think and feel, which will allow you to lead them to the emotion that you want them to feel.

Talk clearly

Do not ruin the beauty of your story by telling it in a way that no one understands what you are saying. Therefore, talk clearly. Make sure you pronounce every word correctly. Also, regulate the speed of your speech. Some people tend to talk too fast when telling a story. If you are saying something that is important, then there is no need for you to rush. If you think that it is something that you can talk about quickly, then perhaps it would be better if you just drop it completely and remove it from the story.

Make eye contact

Making eye contact makes the audience feel noticed and valued. Of course, this is only possible if you are working with a small audience where you can look at everybody and establish eye contact. But, eye contact is also important even when you talk to a huge audience. Of course, you cannot be expected to have eye contact with everyone, but at least do so with as many people as you can. Do not forget to act naturally. Make eye contact as you tell your story. It is also a good way to have a more intimate connection with your audience.

Make your own

Make your own story. Creating your own story will give you all the flexibility that you need and control over what you want to tell your audience. Read as many stories as you can, so that you will have an idea of how stories are made. You can also watch many videos online on how storytellers tell their exciting stories in a way that grabs the audience's interest.

Another way to make a story is by developing an already existing story or by viewing a story from a different perspective. Of course, you can always share your real-life experiences as well. In fact, it is advised that even when you share something that is completely imaginary, you can always follow it up with a real-life experience to make the story more convincing and believable. If you look closely, it is actually the other way around: By telling a story, you make the truth more believable. This is true, especially if the fiction story that you share is able to touch the hearts of the audience. It is also common for real-life experiences storyteller to exaggerate his experiences in order to come up with a better story. Now, be careful about exaggerating a story, especially if you claim it to be something that you have actually experienced yourself. After all, you would not want people to think that you are lying to them.

Change

When it comes to good stories, there is an element that should always be present, and that is the element of change. The character in the story, more specifically, the protagonist, must undergo an internal transformation. Take note that this refers to a change that is internal. This may be a change in the personality of the character or even just a single part of his persona.

Practice

Of course, the best way to learn how to tell stories effectively is to practice it. Tell as many stories as you can to as many people as possible. Do not limit yourself to any rule and try to experiment on what works best for you. It is also worth noting that people may react differently. For example, telling a particular story to person A does not always mean that you can get the same reaction when you tell the same story to person B. Therefore, it is also important that you empathize with your audience to have a better understanding of how they feel. Although you have your story to tell, take some time to stop for a moment and try to view things from your audience's perspective. By doing so, you will have a better understanding of your audience and have a hint on what would work and not.

You can also practice by telling the story to yourself. You may also want to record yourself so that you can listen to it. Pay attention to how you sound like and how you deliver the story. Are there lines that you say too quickly and do you pronounce all the words clearly and properly? Also pay attention to your speed. Effective storytelling should not be too slow or too fast. However, you also cannot maintain the same speed throughout the story; otherwise, it will sound too boring.

Know different stories for different emotions

Do you want to be ready with a story for every human emotion? Then prepare. One's preparation is important to effective sympathetic storytelling. Know different stories for the different human emotions. For example, for today, read some stories that deal with sadness. Tomorrow, you can read stories about love, and so on. Come to think of it, there are not so many human emotions to deal with. In less than five months' time, you will already have lots of stories under your belt that will allow you to tell a story on any occasion.

Take note that you do not have to memorize the stories. In fact, there are many sympathetic storytellers out there who only have story ideas and simply improvise as they tell a story. Hence, you do not have to memorize every word of the story. Once you get used to telling stories, you will be surprised just how easy it is to tell a story even if you only have ideas about the story. You can easily improvise when needed. Sometimes it is also helpful to edit some parts of a story to make it more personal and relevant to your audience. Even simple changes as using the name of one of your audience can make your story be more interesting.

Do not dictate to your audience what to do

Even if you are to deliver a persuasive speech, you should not dictate your audience what to do. After all, no one wants to just follow the dictates of anyone blindly. Instead, you should show to your audience the benefits of your chosen position and make them decide for themselves. Of course, this rule is not absolute.

Sometimes you need to be direct; however, do not make your audience feel as if you are commanding them to do something. The best way to persuade people is not by using commands but by inspiring them to make decisions for themselves. Make them think and feel that they want to do what you want. Of course, using stories is one of the best ways to do this.

Ask

You do not need to be a mind reader just to understand the person you are talking to. Remember that you can always ask questions to have a better understanding of your audience. Of course, when you ask something, you should also learn how to listen. Listen not only to the answers but also pay attention to gestures and tone of voice of your audience or any person whom you are talking with. People are usually open when you ask the right questions. This is true, especially when engaged in any social interaction. Take note that the more you understand the person with whom you are talking to, the more easily you will know the right story to tell. Sometimes all you have to do is ask questions in order to make someone open up so that you can sympathize with him. Of course, this also presents an opportunity for you to tell a story that your audience can empathize with. Just remember, if you find it hard to tell what story would best empathize with your audience, do not hesitate to ask questions. Your first goal is to have a good understanding of your audience in order for you to effectively sympathize with them.

Proper delivery

Even if you have one of the greatest stories to tell, it will not be as effective if it is not properly delivered. Learning to deliver a story is important to a storyteller; simply having a good story is not enough. If you watch and listen to professional storytellers, you will notice that sometimes the stories that they share are nothing new, just typical ones that almost anyone can tell. However, the way they deliver the story is where the magic turns an average story into something that is really worth listening to.

But, what is the proper way to deliver a story? Again, the story must flow smoothly. You should know it by heart so that it will be easier for you to talk about it. The tone of your voice is also important, as well as your gestures. Simply by paying attention to your audience, a connection is formed. Instead of just "telling" the story, tell it in a way as if you were directly talking to your audience.

Learn to use pauses

Many people who tell stories commit the common mistake of talking continuously and even too fast. You should learn to pause from time to time. Use it wisely. A pause can help build up the suspense and the story. Sometimes you will also have to pause in order give enough time for the audience to process information. So, how do you use pauses effectively?

If you are invited to tell a story to a large audience, you can start by being silent. Just pause for a while and make eye contact. Believe it or not, this is actually a good way to capture the attention of your audience. You can be rest assured that they will be most attentive to you the moment you talk. This is also a good way to get comfortable and relaxed, especially if you are not used to talking in front of a crowd.

When you pause, your role changes from the one who is talking to the one who is listening. It is a good way to listen to the reaction of your audience. This is true, especially when you mention something funny or simply to give time for a meaningful statement to sink in.

A pause can also be used to add emphasis or for the audience to feel more that "aha" moment, or simply as a way to give time for the audience to laugh. Another important use of a pause that is not realized by many is that it allows your audience to enjoy the imaginary world that you have created for them. Let them dream their own dreams and draw their own conclusions out of the visions that you evoked.

Build anticipation

Anticipation creates a powerful pressure and exciting points that the audience can hang on as the beauty of the story slowly unfolds before them. Everybody loves a story that brings them to the edge of their seat and looks forward to something special. Storytellers build anticipation and leave the audience hanging for a brief period, especially during the exciting points in a story in order to give the audience the pleasure to enjoy the moment.

Smooth transition of events

As a storyteller, you should avoid transitioning from one part of a story to another too quickly. This can be confusing for your audience, which can prevent them from understanding what you are trying to say. The problem is that if they miss some parts of your story, they may no longer understand it or appreciate it fully. Be sure to transition smoothly from one event to another, and give enough time for your audience to "tune in" to every development in the story.

Be more human

When you use sympathetic storytelling, you will realize that what actually makes a good story is when it is "more human." When it comes to being human, one of the main things that you should focus on is one's emotion. Yes, a story can take place in outer space. In fact, a story may not even have any human character, but you can instill human ideas and emotions into the story to make it meaningful. Therefore, if you want to come up with the next bestselling story, a story that people will love, then you should focus on crafting a story that touches on a specific human emotion or nature. Unfortunately, some people think that extraordinary stories require something that is outside the realm of being a human. This is not true. In fact, if it were so, then it would be a story that nobody will understand. Therefore, when you make your own story, remember to get in touch with your nature as a human being, especially with your emotions. It is true that people can be different from one another. A person may have different physical features than others. It is also common for people to have different opinions and views. However, everyone, whether young or old, rich or poor, knows the truthfulness of any emotion, such as the feeling of happiness, love, fear, pain, and others. There is truth in every human emotion because it is something that you feel, without any need of logic or reason. Any particular emotion is known to any man in the same way it is known to any other. Love is love; pain is pain. It is in the seat of human emotion that the truth that everyone cannot deny because they can feel it.

Be an inspiration

Use your stories to inspire. Stories have the power to communicate into the hearts and minds of the people. There are stories that teach love and kindness, while there are also those that promote twisted values and morality. It is up to the storytellers to draw the line and decide where they stand. Stories infuse the world with so much power and magic that they have a strong influence on the people. May your stories be an inspiration that will promote the greater good.

Conclusion

Thanks for making it through to the end of this book. We hope it was informative and able to provide you with all of the tools you need to achieve your goals whatever they may be.

The next step is to apply everything that you have learned. By now, you should already know the beauty and power of sympathetic storytelling. Take note of this subtle skill and art, whatever you speak or try to send a message, practice and call on it as much as possible. Making it a natural part of your thinking and talking. You just have to harness and develop it. With consistent practice, you will be able to tell a wonderful story that can touch the hearts of many human being. That is the true path to great success.

Sympathetic storytelling has a power that can create lasting effects and changes. Therefore, you should be careful how you use it. Somehow, it can be said that stories set the direction of humanity. This is because stories can change how people think. As such, they can change people. A world that is full of positive stories trends towards a bright future, while a world that is full of bad or negative stories may be a prophecy of its own destruction. As a sympathetic storyteller, it is up to you to create a world through your stories to which the material world can pattern itself. You do not just talk and recite a story; rather, you communicate directly into the hearts and minds of your audience. From this perspective, it can be said that storytelling is a sensitive art that can have truly powerful and material effects. May your stories be a source of light that can overthrow the darkness.

Finally, if you found this book useful in any way, a review on Amazon is always appreciated!

www.ingramcontent.com/pod-product-compliance
Lightning Source LLC
Chambersburg PA
CBHW050020230526
45470CB00003B/1048